Original title:
Building Love That Lasts

Copyright © 2024 Swan Charm
All rights reserved.

Author: Eliora Lumiste
ISBN HARDBACK: 978-9916-89-055-4
ISBN PAPERBACK: 978-9916-89-056-1
ISBN EBOOK: 978-9916-89-057-8

Seasons of Trust

In springtime bloom, we start anew,
With whispered promises, so fresh and true.
The summer sun, it warms our hearts,
In laughter's glow, together we part.

As autumn leaves begin to fall,
We gather close, we heed the call.
With winter's chill, we find our way,
In trust, we stand, come what may.

Unbreakable Threads

In gentle hands, we weave our dreams,
With every stitch, a bond it seems.
Through trials faced, and laughter shared,
Our hearts entwined, a love declared.

From golden dawns to starry nights,
Through every storm, in all our fights.
These threads of gold, they cannot fray,
Together strong, we'll always stay.

The House of Us

In walls of stone, our laughter rings,
A sacred space where love takes wing.
With open doors and warmth inside,
In every room, our hearts abide.

Through every season, storms may roar,
We build our dreams forevermore.
In simple joys, we find our bliss,
In every hug, a gentle kiss.

Gardens of Devotion

In quiet corners, flowers grow,
With tender care, our love will show.
Roots intertwined, beneath the earth,
In every bloom, we find our worth.

With morning light, we rise each day,
In shared moments, we gently sway.
In each petal, whispers sweet,
In this garden, hearts will meet.

Navigating Love's Maze

In shadows deep, we wander slow,
With whispered secrets, hearts aglow.
Paths twist and turn, yet still we tread,
Hand in hand, where love is led.

Unraveling doubts, like threads undone,
Finding solace in the rising sun.
Each step we take, a choice to make,
Together we learn, together we break.

In laughter shared, in quiet sighs,
The map unfolds beneath our eyes.
Through stormy nights and sunny days,
We forge a bond in love's sweet maze.

A Haven of Hope

In the quiet corner, dreams arise,
Beneath the blanket of soft blue skies.
A sanctuary where hearts can heal,
Where whispers of comfort gently appeal.

Through stormy tempests, we stand tall,
In the embrace of love, we never fall.
A refuge found, where tears subside,
In this haven, hope will always abide.

When shadows linger, and fears take flight,
We light the candles, igniting the night.
Together we rise, never alone,
In the garden of faith, love's seeds are sown.

Choreography of Caring

In every glance, we dance a rhyme,
With gentle steps, we weave through time.
An elegant waltz, a tender embrace,
The rhythm of life, at our own pace.

With every touch, a story unfolds,
Of laughter and warmth, and hands we hold.
In the quiet moments, we find our beat,
A beautiful song, where souls meet.

As seasons change, and time may sway,
Our hearts remain in perfect display.
The choreography of love's sweet art,
Dances forever in every heart.

Lifelong Adventures

On paths unknown, where echoes call,
We chase the wonders, never small.
In every sunrise, a chance to roam,
Together we build our dreams, our home.

From mountains high to valleys low,
In whispered dreams, together we grow.
Each twist and turn, a tale to share,
In our lifelong journey, love is rare.

With every step, a world unfolds,
In laughter and courage, our story holds.
Through trials faced and joys we create,
Our lifelong adventure awaits, it's fate.

The Dance of Commitment

In the twilight glow, we take our stand,
Hearts entwined, united hand in hand.
With every heartbeat, our promise rings,
In the dance of trust, our love takes wings.

Through storms and trials, we'll find our grace,
In the arms of time, we'll find our place.
Each step together, a story we weave,
In this tapestry of love, we believe.

With every whisper, our souls ignite,
In the moonlit glow, everything feels right.
The rhythm of us, a beautiful sound,
In this dance of commitment, our love is found.

Echoes of Forever

In the silence, memories softly play,
Whispers of love that will never decay.
Every glance shared, a promise remained,
In the echoes of forever, hearts unchained.

With voices entwined, we sing as one,
In the warmth of the night, our fears come undone.
A melody crafted from laughter and tears,
In this song of forever, we conquer our fears.

As seasons change and the years drift by,
In the depths of our love, we learn to fly.
With hope as our guide, we reach for the sun,
In the echoes of forever, we will run.

The Path We Forge

In the journey we take, each step feels right,
With dreams as our compass, we light up the night.
Through valleys we wander, on mountains we climb,
Together we'll flourish, transcending all time.

The road may be winding, yet still, we embrace,
With laughter and love, we quicken our pace.
Every turn brings us closer, hearts linked as one,
On the path we forge, our souls are undone.

In the beauty of moments, hand in hand we tread,
With courage as armor, we conquer our dread.
In the tapestry woven, our stories align,
On the path that we forge, your heart is mine.

A Symphony of Souls

In the quiet of dusk, our spirits collide,
Creating a harmony, side by side.
With each gentle note, our love intertwines,
In this symphony of souls, pure joy defines.

As the stars twinkle bright in the velvet sky,
Our music resounds, allowing hearts to fly.
With laughter as a score, sweet melodies bloom,
In this symphony of souls, love finds its room.

So let the world fade, let the moment extend,
With passion and grace, on us, we depend.
In this endless concert, our spirits will rise,
In the symphony of souls, we touch the skies.

The Palette of Our Days

Each sunrise spills a hue,
A canvas born anew.
With every laugh and tear,
We paint our memories dear.

The softest shades of blue,
In twilight's gentle view.
Emerald fields of grace,
The warmth of love's embrace.

Golden rays of joy,
In moments we employ.
Violet whispers at night,
Starlit dreams take flight.

Every color tells a tale,
In winds that softly sail.
Through storms, we find our way,
United in our stay.

So let us blend and blend,
With each brush, hearts extend.
This palette, rich and wide,
Where life's great truths abide.

In the Shade of Togetherness

Beneath the ancient tree,
We find our sanctuary.
In whispers, secrets grow,
As gentle breezes flow.

The world fades far away,
In this sweet hideaway.
With laughter filling space,
It's love that we embrace.

The sun may rise and fall,
Yet here we stand, enthralled.
In shadows long and deep,
Our bond is ours to keep.

Time dances as we share,
Each moment, pure and rare.
We weave our stories tight,
In harmony's soft light.

Forever we'll remain,
Together, joy and pain.
In the shade, hand in hand,
A love that will withstand.

Weaving Dreams with Time

In the loom of twilight,
We spin our hopes so bright.
Threads of gold and silver,
In patterns that will quiver.

Each dream, a tapestry,
Woven naturally.
Moments stitched with care,
In the fabric we share.

Time, the guiding hand,
Crafts our stories grand.
With every inch we sew,
Our spirits start to glow.

The past and future blend,
As we begin to mend.
Embroidered with our grace,
In dreams, we find our place.

Together, we align,
In the heart's design.
Weaving love's sweet rhyme,
In the fabric of time.

The Pulse of Promises

In silence, vows are made,
A serenade displayed.
Each heartbeat, strong and clear,
In shadows, love draws near.

We walk a path of trust,
With faith that's pure and just.
Every promise, a strand,
Binding hearts hand in hand.

Through storms, we shall not break,
With every choice we make.
The pulse of dreams alive,
In unity, we strive.

With whispers in the night,
We nurture hope's soft light.
Together, we will rise,
With passion in our eyes.

For every word we share,
Resounding in the air.
The pulse of love's refrain,
Together, we remain.

The Light of Lasting Connection

In shadows deep, where silence sighs,
We weave our dreams beneath the skies.
With every glance, a spark ignites,
Our hearts entwined in gentle lights.

Through stormy nights, we'll find our way,
In whispered words, our fears allay.
No distance bends the bond we share,
Our souls united, strong and rare.

In laughter's glow, in tears' sweet grace,
We forge a truth time can't erase.
Each moment shared, a treasure kept,
In love's embrace, our spirits leapt.

With every heartbeat, every breath,
We conquer doubt, we conquer death.
Together long, with hope anew,
Our light will guide, forever true.

So let us dance through life's vast sea,
In perfect harmony, you and me.
For in this bond, we shall not wane,
The light of love will always reign.

Our Intimate Tomorrow

Beneath the stars, we'll chart our course,
With dreams in hand and quiet force.
As morning breaks, our futures blend,
In every moment, love will tend.

With laughter's song, we'll greet the day,
As hopes arise and fears give way.
In whispered promises, hearts confide,
Together, always, side by side.

Through trials faced and joys embraced,
In every challenge, we're interlaced.
The path ahead, a canvas bright,
We'll paint our dreams in colors light.

In gentle strokes, our lives combine,
With every touch, our souls align.
A tapestry of love unfurls,
Our intimate tomorrow swirls.

So take my hand, let futures gleam,
In rhythm, dance to love's sweet theme.
With every heartbeat, we will know,
Together, dear, we'll always grow.

The Blueprint of Belonging

In the quiet corners of our hearts,
A map unfolds where love imparts.
Lines connecting near and far,
Each stitch a sign, each mark a star.

In laughter shared, in tears we weave,
A tapestry, we dare believe.
Roots entwined in sacred ground,
In every heartbeat, home is found.

Together we build with steady hands,
A structure strong, where understanding stands.
Each brick a story, each beam a dream,
In the blueprint drawn, we find our theme.

Through storms that rage and winds that howl,
We'll stay steadfast, our hearts a prowl.
For in this space, we dare to grow,
Within the warmth of love's soft glow.

Walls of Warmth

Brick by brick, we stand so tall,
Built on trust, we will not fall.
These walls embraced through every strife,
A sanctuary, a shared life.

Colors soft, like whispers sweet,
In this haven, our souls meet.
Laughter lingers in every room,
Filling our hearts, dispelling gloom.

In shadows cast by evening light,
We gather close, our spirits bright.
With open arms, we let love in,
Building walls where hope begins.

Every crack tells stories dear,
Memories forged through joy and fear.
In these walls, our dreams take flight,
Forever bound by love's pure light.

The Frame of Forever

Within this frame, our moments shine,
Captured whispers, yours and mine.
Every glance, a brush of fate,
Timeless love, we celebrate.

In silver edges, stories gleam,
Framed in laughter, a perfect dream.
Through seasons change, our colors blend,
In this portrait, love transcends.

An open door, a warm embrace,
In the frame, we find our place.
Every smile, a snapshot bright,
In this canvas, we take flight.

Together painted against time's flow,
In the masterpiece, our hearts aglow.
Forever cherished, forever true,
In every frame, it's me and you.

Echoes of Endless Devotion

In the silent whispers of the night,
Your name echoes, a soft delight.
Through every shadow, a gentle call,
In love's embrace, we'll never fall.

Moments shared, like stars above,
Each twinkle tells of endless love.
With every heartbeat, we find our song,
A melody where we belong.

Through trials faced, we find our way,
In each sunrise, a brand new day.
With hands entwined, our spirits soar,
In the echoes, we seek more.

Forever bound, through thick and thin,
In every loss, in every win.
These echoes resonate, strong and true,
In the symphony of me and you.

Crafting an Unseen Bridge

In silence, whispers weave the thread,
Between us lies a path unsaid.
With gentleness, our hearts align,
Creating bonds, both pure and fine.

Through storms we will not drift apart,
Each beat resounds a hopeful start.
Together, we shall dare to leap,
Across the chasm, wide and deep.

With every step, our faith shall grow,
In twilight's glow, we'll surely know.
The bridge we craft is one of trust,
In dreams we tread, the unseen gust.

Though shadows linger near and far,
We'll find our guiding, glowing star.
With laughter shared, our spirits rise,
As bridges form beneath the skies.

So hand in hand, let's move ahead,
With courage bold, let love be spread.
In unity, we'll face the roar,
And craft a bridge forevermore.

Sturdy Steps into Tomorrow

With sturdy steps, we pave the way,
Each moment sewn, a bright display.
Together we shall carve our path,
With strength that flows, a gentle wrath.

The sun will rise, and shadows cast,
Yet forward, we will hold steadfast.
With every footfall, dreams take flight,
In unity, we seek the light.

Though doubts may whisper in the night,
Our hearts entwined, we'll find the might.
Through valleys deep, we'll rise again,
With faith as sturdy as the rain.

Tomorrow's dawn, a canvas clear,
With colors bold, we'll paint our cheer.
Each step we take, with hope aligned,
In every heartbeat, love defined.

So let us walk, no fear to show,
Into the dawn, where wildflowers grow.
With sturdy steps and hearts aglow,
We journey forth, our future's flow.

Harmonizing Our Dreams

With gentle tunes, our dreams unite,
In harmony, we find our flight.
Each note a wish, each chord a spark,
Together, we shall light the dark.

The rhythm flows like river's bend,
With every turn, our souls transcend.
In vivid hues, our voices blend,
Creating paths that never end.

With whispered hopes, we rise anew,
Our dreams entwined, a vibrant view.
In every heartbeat, music flows,
In perfect time, our passion grows.

So hand in hand, let's strum aloud,
In gratitude, we'll sing so proud.
Each dream a verse, our hearts the song,
In harmonies, we all belong.

Together, let's create the space,
Where dreams take root, then find their grace.
In melodies that softly gleam,
We harmonize, fulfill our dream.

Heartfelt Foundations

In quiet corners, love is laid,
A structure strong, with care displayed.
Each brick a memory, gently placed,
In heart's embrace, our dreams are traced.

Through trials faced, we shape our home,
With warmth and laughter, we have grown.
Together built, our fortress stands,
United still, in gentle hands.

With every stone, a story told,
In joy and heartache, brave and bold.
Foundations firm, our spirits soar,
With every step, we yearn for more.

In twilight's glow, we find our peace,
The love we share will never cease.
With every dawn, our hopes align,
In heartfelt steadfast, we entwine.

Through storms that rage, we stand as one,
In every shadow, light is spun.
With heartfelt dreams, we forge ahead,
In love's embrace, no fear or dread.

Stars in Our Sky

Twinkling lights in the night,
Guiding dreams with their spark.
Each a wish whispered low,
A beacon in the dark.

Together we gaze, in awe,
Connecting hearts by the light.
In silence we share our hopes,
Stars shining through the night.

The vastness holds our secrets,
Stories told in glowing hues.
In constellations we find peace,
Wonders in every view.

With every wish that we make,
A bond forms beneath the glow.
Forever in this moment,
Together we will grow.

Underneath this endless sky,
We share the dreams we sigh.
In the dance of starlit night,
Our spirits learn to fly.

A Canvas of Companionship

Colors blend in soft embrace,
Each stroke tells a tale untold.
Upon this canvas we create,
Friendship painted bold.

Hand in hand we mix our shades,
Laughter echoes in the air.
Every hue a memory made,
Love is the brush we share.

With every shade of laughter,
And every tear we dry,
Together we paint our journey,
As time passes by.

In the gallery of our lives,
Each moment holds its grace.
Our hearts, a canvas woven tight,
In this sacred space.

Through storms and sunny weather,
Our bond will not erase.
A masterpiece forever bright,
In the art of embrace.

Threads of Time

In the loom where memories bind,
Threads of moments woven tight.
Each strand holds a story true,
Crafted under moon's soft light.

As seasons change and time flows,
We stitch our dreams with care.
With every thread, our journey grows,
In this tapestry we share.

Through laughter, joy, and sorrow,
Each fiber tells a tale.
Woven through the night and day,
Our bond will never fail.

The fabric of our lives unspools,
With each stitch, our lives we trace.
In every moment, love unfolds,
As time leaves not a trace.

Together we weave our future,
In colors bright and rare.
A true reflection of our hearts,
Threads of time laid bare.

Creating Patterns of Peace

In a world of noise and haste,
We find a silent space.
Through gentle thoughts and actions,
We weave a calming grace.

Patterns form like ripples wide,
In hearts, a tranquil tune.
Each act of kindness shown,
Brings harmony like the moon.

Gathered in this sacred still,
We breathe and feel the light.
Creating peace with every breath,
Together shining bright.

Our hands joined in unity,
With purpose in our hearts.
We craft a world of beauty,
Where love never departs.

Let's stitch the seams of kindness,
In patterns bold and free.
A tapestry of friendship,
Creating harmony.

Weaving Threads of Togetherness

In the loom of life we stand,
Threads of joy slip through our hands.
Colors bright in every hue,
Woven dreams, just me and you.

Every stitch a shared delight,
Binding hearts with purest light.
Together in this dance we weave,
A tapestry none can believe.

Moments stitched in laughter's thread,
Whispers soft where angels tread.
In each knot, our secrets blend,
In this fabric, love won't end.

Through silver nights and golden days,
Our woven paths in countless ways.
In harmony, we stand as one,
A masterpiece when all is done.

Threads of life, a sacred pact,
In togetherness, we never lack.
With every twist, our love expands,
Together strong, forever hand in hand.

Pillars of the Heart

In the stillness, heartbeats speak,
Pillars rise where dreams can peak.
Anchored deep in love's embrace,
Standing firm, our sacred space.

Walls of trust and love defined,
In this shelter, souls entwined.
Through the storm, we hold our ground,
In each other, strength is found.

Echoes of laughter fill the air,
Pillars strong, we're always there.
Support and joy in every part,
Building up the fragile heart.

Rooted firm in shared intent,
Every moment, time well spent.
Together we shall never part,
Endless love, our work of art.

As seasons change, we still believe,
In this home, our hearts achieve.
Pillars stand against the night,
Guiding us toward the light.

Timeless Embrace

In whispers soft, time fades away,
Moments dance, an endless play.
In your arms, forever mine,
A timeless love we redefine.

Seasons pass, yet we remain,
In each heartbeat, joy and pain.
Through every tear, through every smile,
We'll entangle life's long mile.

Memories paint our canvas bright,
Colors clash, yet feel just right.
In this embrace, we're not alone,
In your warmth, I've found my home.

Time may stretch, yet hearts unite,
In this love, we find our light.
Every second, a sweet caress,
In your gaze, I find my rest.

Eternal souls, forever free,
In each moment, just you and me.
With every breath, our legacy,
A timeless bond, our tapestry.

Crafting a Tapestry of Us

With every thread, a story told,
In our hands, a future bold.
Stitched with care, our dreams align,
Crafted hearts, a design divine.

Patterns shift, yet roots remain,
Together dancing through the rain.
In every loop, our laughter sings,
A tapestry of wondrous things.

Colors blend as passions mix,
In this art, love's gentle tricks.
Every angle, every seam,
We create an endless dream.

Through trials faced, we thread the path,
In the warmth of love's sweet wrath.
Every turn, we hold the trust,
Crafting memories, creating us.

In the fabric of our days,
Woven tight in countless ways.
Together here, we stitch it true,
This masterpiece is me and you.

Relentless Sunsets

The sky ablaze in fiery hues,
Golden rays bid day adieu.
Clouds like wisps in twilight dance,
Nature's art, a fleeting glance.

Shadows stretch, embrace the night,
While stars emerge, a silver light.
Each moment captured, time stands still,
In every dusk, the heart does thrill.

Transience weaves its gentle thread,
In beauty's grasp, we feel the fed.
Relentless scenes of calm and grace,
In sunsets, we find our place.

Horizon whispers tales untold,
Of sunsets cherished, dreams unfold.
In every hue, a story spun,
Reflecting hopes when day is done.

Yet still we chase the daylight's end,
For in each fade, new dreams ascend.
A promise made with every dusk,
Relentless love, in time we trust.

The Heart's Blueprint

In whispered tones, the heart reveals,
The map of love, the path it seals.
Each beat a guide, a gentle sigh,
Through valleys deep and mountains high.

Connections woven, thread by thread,
In every joy, in every dread.
The blueprint drawn by hands unseen,
In every tear, in every dream.

With laughter's echo, pain's caress,
The heart will shape our happiness.
Lines intertwine like rivers flow,
In every rhythm, we come to know.

A dance of souls, an artful play,
In this grand scheme, we find our way.
The heart's design, both strong and frail,
In every love, we shall prevail.

So heed the pulsing, fierce and true,
Embrace the map that leads to you.
For in the heart's eternal quest,
We carve our names; we are blessed.

Everlasting Footprints

In sands of time, our stories lie,
Each footprint soft, a whisper shy.
Seas may wash and winds may shift,
Yet traces linger, memories gift.

Through fields of green and mountains tall,
Our steps have echoed, one and all.
In laughter shared and tears we cried,
Everlasting bonds, forever tied.

Every journey starts anew,
With paths unknown, a vibrant view.
Yet every step, both bold and meek,
Leaves lasting marks we yearn to seek.

In twilight's glow, reflections gleam,
Of lives entwined, of shared esteem.
The footprints fade but love remains,
In every heart, its sweet refrains.

So as we wander, hand in hand,
Across this boundless, wondrous land,
We'll treasure each, both small and grand,
For everlasting footprints stand.

Winds of Understanding

Across the fields, the whispers flow,
Carried forth by winds that know.
They speak of truths both soft and bright,
In every gust, a spark of light.

With every breeze, the world exclaims,
To shed our doubts, to share our names.
In understanding, hearts unite,
Awakening dreams in shared delight.

Through trials faced and storms endured,
The winds will guide, our souls assured.
In every gust, a lesson waits,
To greet each moment, embrace our fates.

So let the winds of change arise,
To teach us love, to open eyes.
In understanding's gentle sway,
We'll find our strength and light the way.

Together, bound by hope's sweet call,
With every breeze, we rise and fall.
In life's great dance, hand in hand,
We'll learn the language of this land.

The Labyrinth of Longing

In shadows deep where whispers play,
A heart wanders, lost in the fray.
Memories echo, soft as a sigh,
Beneath a moonlit, starry sky.

Paths entwined, a maze of dreams,
Each corner turned, or so it seems.
Hope flickers like a distant flame,
Yet fear and love share one sweet name.

A touch of warmth, a fleeting glance,
In this dance of fate, we take our chance.
Yet longing lingers, a bittersweet song,
In the labyrinth, where we belong.

Time weaves glances, threads of fate,
In the silence, we contemplate.
With every heartbeat, the world expands,
Drawing closer with trembling hands.

Finding solace in the unknown,
In this twisted path, we're never alone.
As echoes fade, new tales are spun,
In the labyrinth, two hearts are one.

Sketches of Serenity

Beneath the trees where shadows fall,
Gentle breezes softly call.
Whispers mingle with the leaves,
In this haven, the spirit weaves.

Colors blend, a painter's dream,
Serenity flows like a quiet stream.
As sunlight dances on the ground,
In each moment, peace is found.

Each petal holds a tale untold,
In quiet corners, the heart is bold.
Sketching skies in shades of blue,
Where time stands still, and hopes renew.

A canvas wide, the mind takes flight,
In gentle hues, both soft and light.
As daylight fades to twilight's call,
The soul finds solace, cradled by all.

In this gallery of dreams serene,
Life's true beauty can be seen.
Here, we gather, hand in hand,
Sketching peace on sacred land.

Cradling Tomorrow

In the dawn's gentle embrace,
Hope ignites, a tender space.
With every heartbeat, futures grow,
Cradling dreams, our spirits flow.

The horizon whispers soft and clear,
Every moment, drawing near.
With open arms, we welcome change,
In this dance, our hearts arrange.

Stars align in a cosmic dance,
Guiding us with a fearless glance.
Through shadows deep, we find our light,
In the unknown, we take our flight.

With every breath, a promise blooms,
In the silence, ambition looms.
Together we reach, our hands entwine,
Cradling tomorrow, your heart in mine.

As the sun rises, painting the day,
In love's embrace, we choose to stay.
With every step, a brighter road,
Cradling tomorrow, together we behold.

A Nest of Our Making

In the warmth of shared delight,
We build a nest in fading light.
With threads of laughter, soft and bright,
We weave our dreams in endless flight.

Branches stretch, embracing the sky,
Where love blossoms, we learn to fly.
Every moment, pure and true,
In this haven, it's me and you.

Gentle whispers, secrets shared,
In this nest, we are declared.
Home is not just walls and beams,
But the love that flows in our dreams.

Through storms and trials, we stand tall,
In our nest, we can never fall.
With wings wide open, hearts embrace,
A sanctuary, our sacred space.

As seasons change, our roots will grow,
In the quiet stillness, love will flow.
Nestled close, we find our place,
A nest of our making, time won't erase.

Unwavering Bonds

In silence we stand, hand in hand,
Through storms that may come, we understand.
Roots intertwined in the soil of trust,
In the fire of life, it's love that we must.

Through laughter and tears, our spirits entwined,
In the tapestry woven, our hearts combined.
No distance can sever, no time can erase,
In the heart's quiet chambers, you find your place.

Facing the world, we rise side by side,
In the warmth of our shelter, no fear can abide.
The journey is long, yet together we stride,
With unwavering bonds, there's nothing to hide.

Under the stars, our dreams take their flight,
A compass of hope that guides us each night.
In the strength of our union, we find our way,
A beacon of love that won't fade away.

With whispers of promise, we'll venture ahead,
In the book of our lives, love's pages are spread.
The ink may grow faded, yet never the heart,
For woven together, we'll never depart.

Love Like Infinite Stars

In the night sky, your light shines bright,
Infinite stars reflecting our delight.
Like constellations, our stories align,
In the cosmos of love, our hearts intertwine.

Each glance a spark, igniting the dark,
On this boundless journey, you are my mark.
Galaxies swirling, our passions ignite,
With you by my side, the world feels just right.

Through the vastness, we dance, we soar,
Each heartbeat a whisper, we yearn for more.
In the tapestry of night, let's weave our dreams,
In love's woven fabric, nothing redeems.

Like comets that blaze, we leave our trace,
A celestial bond in this infinite space.
With hope in our eyes, we navigate time,
With love like the stars, forever we climb.

So let's chart our course through the moonlit waves,
In the arms of forever, our souls are our saves.
With each twinkle above, our promises flow,
In this universe vast, it's love that we know.

Moments Chiseled in Time

In the quiet dawn, moments unfold,
Whispers of memories, stories retold.
Each heartbeat a chisel, sculpting our fate,
Carved in the fabric, we patiently wait.

In laughter and joy, time bends and sways,
Painting our lives in vibrant arrays.
With each passing second, our canvas expands,
A masterpiece woven by tender hands.

Through the seasons we wander, hand in hand,
In the realm of forever, together we stand.
Every glance captured, each touch profound,
In these fleeting moments, love's echoes resound.

As twilight descends, shadows grow long,
We gather the memories, like notes in a song.
In the depths of our hearts, these treasures reside,
Moments chiseled in time, where love can't divide.

So let's hold these instants, embrace what we find,
In the art of existence, our spirits entwined.
For time is a river, flowing with grace,
In the journey we share, we have found our place.

Crafting Our Tomorrow

With gentle hands, we mold our fate,
Dreams unfolding at a deliberate rate.
In the canvas of time, together we draw,
Crafting our tomorrow, with love as the law.

Each moment a brushstroke, vivid and bright,
Painting our journey with colors of light.
With whispers of hope, we sketch what's to be,
Creating a future, just you and me.

Through challenges faced, we rise ever tall,
In the face of the storm, we'll conquer it all.
With laughter our guide, and courage our friend,
In the story of life, our hearts will transcend.

In the garden of dreams, we plant every seed,
With patience and love, we nourish each need.
As seasons will change, our blossoms will grow,
In the warmth of our love, together we'll glow.

So let us envision a world yet unseen,
With threads of compassion, together we'll weave.
In crafting our tomorrow, hand in hand we stand,
Creating a legacy, forever planned.

Celebrating Every Beat

In the rhythm of our hearts,
Life's melody unfolds.
Each moment a sweet dance,
A story yet untold.

We gather joy like blossoms,
In fields of gold we play.
Every laugh, a note in time,
Crafting bright arrays.

With every breath, a heartbeat,
A note in love's sweet song.
Together, deep in feeling,
We find where we belong.

As stars light up the night,
Our spirits soar high and free.
Celebrating every beat,
In perfect harmony.

Life's concert plays forever,
In the music we create.
Each beat a step toward joy,
Together, we celebrate.

Foundations of Forever

Built with whispers and dreams,
The past weaves through the now.
Strong as roots in the soil,
We'll share our sacred vow.

Every brick a memory,
Every stone a shared glance.
Together, we construct trust,
In love's enduring dance.

Layers deep in affection,
We find shelter from the storm.
Hand in hand, we will weather,
In each other, keep warm.

Brick by brick, we'll build high,
With love as our design.
Foundations forged in laughter,
In moments, intertwine.

Through challenges and triumphs,
We lay the paths we tread.
In the heart's strong structure,
Forever, we will tread.

The Architecture of Affection

In arches made of kindness,
And walls of softest light,
We sketch a world of comfort,
Where love feels warm and bright.

With every touch a blueprint,
Our laughter builds the space.
The architecture of affection,
A masterpiece of grace.

Together we create rooms,
Where hearts can learn to play.
Designs of sweet connection,
In love's perfect array.

Through windows, rays of kindness,
Illuminate our days,
Each pillar holds a story,
In every glance, always.

In the garden of emotions,
We plant seeds of trust and care.
The architecture of affection,
A treasure we will share.

Edges of Eternity

At the brink of forever,
Where time meets open skies,
We dance on dreams and whispers,
And soar where spirit flies.

Each moment, a soft echo,
In the vastness of the night.
Held in waves of gentle starlight,
Our dreams bask in the light.

In the silence, we discover,
What ages cannot fade.
The edges of eternity,
A path of love well laid.

We chase the winds of forever,
Eyes fixed on endless grace.
Together, hand in hand,
We've carved our sacred space.

As we walk this tender line,
Toward horizons far and wide,
Love will guide us through the dark,
With hope as our true guide.

Cultivating Kindness

In the garden of our days,
Seeds of kindness we shall sow,
Nurtured by gentle hearts,
Watch love and warmth gently grow.

A smile shared lights the way,
In shadows, it brings the sun,
Small acts weave a soft web,
Together, we shall run.

When words are kind, wounds heal,
Bridges built with care and grace,
Our hands reach out to hold,
In unity, we find our place.

With every gesture, we learn,
Compassion echoes ever wide,
In this dance of humanity,
Let kindness be our guide.

As we cultivate with love,
A harvest rich, a shared delight,
May the fruits of joy abound,
Kindness spreads both day and night.

Heartstrings Intertwined

Two souls meet on paths aligned,
A melody flows, soft and true,
In every glance, a story shines,
Heartstrings intertwined anew.

In laughter shared, our spirits soar,
Through whispers soft, the night unfolds,
Every moment, a woven lore,
In the warmth, our love enfolds.

Through trials faced, we stand as one,
Hand in hand, we find our way,
In the evening's gentle sun,
Together, we embrace each day.

With dreams entwined like vines of green,
We build a future, bold and bright,
In this bond, we find our scene,
A canvas painted with pure light.

For love's sweet song, we will compose,
In symphonies that never fade,
With every beat, our hearts will choose,
In our harmony, we are made.

Navigating the Years

As time flows by like a river,
Each moment, a precious gem,
We sail on with hearts aglow,
Navigating life's grand diadem.

Through seasons bright and storms that roar,
We gather strength from the past,
Lessons learned, tales to explore,
Building bridges that ever last.

In laughter shared and tears that fall,
Every year a chapter spun,
United, we will stand up tall,
Facing each rising sun.

With friends beside, we chart our course,
Adventure calls, a sweet embrace,
Together, we draw on our source,
In memory's warm, tender space.

Through every twist, our hearts align,
In the tapestry of our days,
With love as our guiding sign,
We celebrate in countless ways.

A Journey of Many Seasons

In whispers of the autumn breeze,
We gather moments, fleeting yet bright,
Each season brings its memories,
Colors that dance in morning light.

From blossoms' bloom to winter's chill,
Life flows through each ebb and tide,
With every change, our hearts we fill,
In the warmth of love, we abide.

Through summer's sun and springtime rain,
We wander paths that twist and turn,
In joy and sorrow, growth remains,
Each lesson taught, a fire that burns.

In the quiet of the twilight glow,
We reflect on the years we've spun,
With every heartbeat, we will know,
Our journey's just begun.

So let us cherish every sight,
The seasons' gifts, both grand and small,
For in this dance, pure and bright,
We find our unity in it all.

The Art of Attachment

In quiet moments, hearts align,
A thread of trust, a gentle sign.
We weave our lives with care and grace,
In every glance, a warm embrace.

Through laughter's echo, shadows sway,
Each whispered secret leads the way.
Together strong, we build and mend,
An artful bond, no start or end.

In storms that rise, we stand as one,
The light of hope, the morning sun.
With every heartbeat, love's refrain,
A canvas rich, where dreams remain.

Through every trial, we find our song,
In unity, we both belong.
A tapestry, both bright and bold,
The art of attachment, joy untold.

So let us dance, let spirits soar,
In each connection, there's so much more.
With open hearts, we revel still,
In the art of attachment, love's sweet thrill.

Echoes of Us

In twilight's glow, memories dwell,
Soft whispers rise, a gentle spell.
The echoes of laughter fill the air,
Reminding us how much we care.

Through winding paths, our footprints trace,
In fleeting moments, we find our place.
Each heartbeat sings of journeys shared,
In echoes of us, love is declared.

As seasons shift, like leaves that fall,
We stand united, through it all.
In shadows cast, we find the light,
Echoes of us, ever so bright.

With every glance, our souls embrace,
In time's embrace, we find our grace.
Together one, we are entwined,
In echoes of us, love is defined.

So let the echoes softly ring,
In every note, our hearts shall sing.
With timeless grace, we rise above,
In echoes of us, the gift of love.

Dreams Interlaced

In quiet nights, our dreams take flight,
Spinning tales beneath the light.
We share our hopes, our wishes bold,
In dreams interlaced, stories unfold.

With every star, we cast our fears,
In silver beams, we find our cheers.
Together weaving visions bright,
In dreams interlaced, hearts ignite.

Through whispered thoughts, our spirits soar,
In shared ambitions, we seek more.
In every promise, we find our place,
In dreams interlaced, love's warm embrace.

As dawn approaches, we chase the day,
With dreams entwined, we'll find our way.
In every challenge, we stand tall,
In dreams interlaced, we'll conquer all.

So let us dream, let hope arise,
In every heartbeat, endless skies.
With passion fierce, we'll carve our path,
In dreams interlaced, we'll find our wrath.

Yesterday, Today, Forever

From yesterday's shadows, lessons gleaned,
In echoes of moments, love's light beamed.
Each chapter written, a part of our tale,
In yesterday's whispers, we shall not fail.

Today unfolds, with promises bright,
We forge our path, with hope in sight.
In laughter's embrace and tender glow,
Today is the moment, love's seeds we sow.

Tomorrow awaits, with dreams to create,
In visions shared, we celebrate fate.
With hands entwined, we face the storm,
In tomorrow's promise, our hearts stay warm.

Through seasons that change, we stand as one,
In every heartbeat, love's journey begun.
Together we walk, hand in hand,
Yesterday, today, in love we stand.

So let time flow, from past to new,
In every moment, I'll cherish you.
Through all of time, forever near,
In yesterday, today, forever dear.

Hearts in Harmony

In the quiet of the night,
Two souls begin to sing.
Melodies entwined,
Creating love's sweet ring.

With every whispered word,
Hearts dance a gentle tune.
Stars sway in the shadows,
Beneath a silver moon.

Harmony of laughter,
Echoes softly in the air.
Hands clasped together,
A bond beyond compare.

Each note a heartbeat shared,
Resonating through the night.
Together they will soar,
In love's enchanting flight.

Through every rise and fall,
Their rhythm stays so true.
Hearts in perfect harmony,
Forever me and you.

The Soundtrack of Us

Every moment we create,
Is a lyric in our song.
Together we compose,
A melody lifelong.

In the starlit evenings,
Our laughter fills the air.
Each note, a memory,
Stringing moments that we share.

The world fades to silence,
When we dance without a care.
In perfect synchrony,
Love's rhythm everywhere.

Through the highs and the lows,
We write our timeless tale.
With every brush of lips,
Through every wind and gale.

So here's to us, my love,
In this soundtrack of delight.
Our hearts will beat as one,
In the soft embrace of night.

Sculpting Our Story

With each gentle touch,
We carve out our dreams.
Chiseling away fear,
Crafting love's shining gleam.

In the light of the dawn,
We shape what's yet to be.
Every moment cherished,
In this gallery of we.

Hands stained with the colors,
Of laughter and of tears.
A masterpiece unfolding,
Across the shifting years.

In silence, we create,
A world uniquely ours.
Every detail speaks love,
Underneath the stars.

Let's mold our forever,
With passion and with grace.
Sculpting our story,
In this sacred space.

Bonds Beyond Time

In the tapestry of fate,
Weaves a thread so bright.
Two hearts intertwined,
Guided by love's light.

Through the sands of time,
We wander hand in hand.
Every twist and turn,
In this endless land.

Memories like treasures,
Stored within our minds.
Our connection so deep,
In the fabric that binds.

As seasons change around,
Love remains constant here.
Bonds beyond the ages,
Ever strong and clear.

So here's to our journey,
A path forever true.
In the book of our lives,
My heart belongs to you.

Harmony in Our Hands

In gentle whispers, hearts unite,
A dance of souls in the soft twilight.
Together we weave, like threads of gold,
A tapestry rich, in stories told.

Each note we share, a melody sweet,
In every heartbeat, our rhythms meet.
With open arms, the world we embrace,
Finding our path in this sacred space.

Through storms we weather, our spirits strong,
In laughter and tears, we know we belong.
With every moment, we kindle the flame,
In harmony's song, love knows no shame.

Let unity guide us, through days and nights,
In every shadow, we find the lights.
Together we'll rise, together we'll stand,
In the timeless song of harmony's hand.

Love's Legacy

In whispers of time, our story unfolds,
A legacy woven, with threads of gold.
Through trials faced and joys we share,
In love's embrace, we find our care.

Each gesture gentle, a timeless spark,
In the depth of night, we light the dark.
With hands held tight, we forge the way,
Love's legacy lives, come what may.

In laughter's echo, in tender grace,
We etch our dreams in every space.
With open hearts, we plant the seeds,
Nurturing futures, fulfilling needs.

As seasons change, our roots run deep,
In memory's garden, our treasures keep.
For love's true essence, forever shall stay,
A legacy written, in every way.

Roots Beneath the Surface

Hidden deep in the ground,
The roots stretch far and wide,
Whispers of what's profound,
In silence they abide.

They drink from ancient springs,
In darkness they entwine,
Strength that nature brings,
A bond that will not shine.

A tapestry unseen,
Connections intertwined,
Between earth and the green,
A legacy defined.

Weathered yet they stand,
In storms, they find their way,
An unbroken strand,
As night surrenders day.

For life is rooted deep,
In hearts and souls it grows,
A promise we must keep,
With what the earth bestows.

The Light in Our Laughter

In joyous bursts we find,
A sparkle in the air,
Laughter unconfined,
Echoing everywhere.

It dances with the breeze,
A flicker in our eyes,
A tune that's sure to please,
A song that never dies.

Through moments big and small,
It lights up every place,
Bringing us through it all,
A warm and bright embrace.

With friends we share the grace,
Of jokes both old and new,
Together we find space,
Where joy is always true.

The light that shows the way,
In shadows, brings us near,
A gift in every play,
Our laughter we hold dear.

In the Cradle of Connection

Where heartbeats softly hum,
And whispers dance in air,
A bond that's just begun,
In moments that we share.

We gather, spirits high,
Around the flames that glow,
With stories soaring sky,
And love that starts to flow.

In silence we can trust,
In presence, warmth ignites,
Connections built on dust,
Transforming dark to light.

Through laughter, tears, and time,
We weave our souls as one,
In rhythms that we rhyme,
A melody begun.

So let us hold this space,
And cherish what is near,
In every soft embrace,
Our hearts will persevere.

Through Storms and Sun

We journey through the gale,
With courage in our chest,
In every gust, we sail,
Through trials, we are blessed.

The sun will break the clouds,
A promise in the skies,
While shadows swirl like shrouds,
We rise, we do not die.

With each drop of the rain,
New life begins to sprout,
In moments full of pain,
We learn what love's about.

Together we will stand,
Against the fiercest storm,
With hope, we take a hand,
Through change, we stay warm.

For life is but a dance,
In cycles we must trust,
Through storms and sun, our chance,
To rise, we are robust.

Foundations of Forever

In whispers soft, our dreams take flight,
Beneath the stars, our hearts unite.
With every step, we build our way,
A bond so deep, it will not sway.

Through trials faced, we stand as one,
A journey grand, yet just begun.
With hands entwined, we face the night,
In love's embrace, we find our light.

The roots we've laid, so strong and true,
In every breath, I cherish you.
As time unfolds, we'll weave our tale,
In echoes sweet, our love won't fail.

With laughter shared and tears we've shed,
We'll carve our path, where dreams are bred.
Together we'll rise, no fear, no dread,
In this foundation, our hearts are fed.

Though storms may come and shadows loom,
Our love will bloom, forever in tune.
In every moment, we'll endure,
For in our hearts, we know we're sure.

The Mosaic of Us

Each piece a story, vibrant and bright,
Together we form a heart's delight.
In colors bold, our lives entwined,
A masterpiece of love defined.

With every laughter, every tear,
We paint the canvas, year by year.
In gentle strokes and bold designs,
Our flaws reveal the best of times.

Through shades of joy and tones of pain,
We find the beauty in the rain.
Every crack, a tale to tell,
In unity, we weave our spell.

Embracing darkness, welcoming light,
In every struggle, we find our might.
Together we'll rise, stronger than ever,
In this mosaic, love is the lever.

So let us dance, and let us sing,
In harmony, together we'll bring
A vibrant world, a life so sweet,
In this mosaic, our hearts will meet.

Anchored Hearts

Like ships that sail through stormy seas,
With anchors strong, we find our peace.
In every tide, our souls are tied,
Together facing the wild ride.

Through winds of change and waves of strife,
We'll weather all, for you are my life.
In tempest's grasp, our bond won't break,
In love's embrace, we are awake.

The lighthouse shines, a guiding light,
With you beside, the dark takes flight.
With steady hands, we'll steer our course,
In every moment, love's our force.

Through ebb and flow, our hearts will soar,
An endless journey, forevermore.
In trust we sail, through storm and calm,
With anchored hearts, we share our balm.

So let the waves crash and winds howl loud,
With you, my love, I stand so proud.
For in this life, our sails will chart,
An endless voyage, anchored hearts.

Through Seasons We Grow

In spring's embrace, we find our way,
With blossoms bright, we greet the day.
In every bud, a promise shines,
In love's sweet bloom, the heart aligns.

As summer's sun warms tender ground,
In laughter's glow, our joys abound.
Through long, warm nights, our spirits soar,
In love's expanse, we yearn for more.

When autumn comes with leaves that fall,
We gather close, we heed the call.
In golden hues, our hearts unite,
With whispered dreams in the fading light.

In winter's frost, when days are bare,
We hold each other, a warmth to share.
In quiet nights, as stars ignite,
Our souls entwined, a love so right.

Through every season, side by side,
In every moment, our hearts abide.
Together we bloom, together we grow,
In life's great dance, our love will flow.

Unbreakable Bonds

Through every storm, we find our way,
With hands held tight, we choose to stay.
In laughter shared, in silence sweet,
Our hearts entwined, we feel complete.

No distance great can dim our light,
Together still, we face the night.
With whispered dreams and hope in sight,
Our spirits soar, our love takes flight.

Each challenge met, together strong,
In rhythm true, we hum our song.
With trust as roots, we grow anew,
In every shade, our bond shines through.

Through thick and thin, forever we stand,
In unity's grasp, we make our plans.
With open hearts, we dare to go,
In love's embrace, we truly grow.

As seasons change, our story's penned,
In every chapter, we transcend.
With laughter, tears; we weave our tale,
In unbreakable bonds, we will prevail.

The Garden of Grace

In every bloom, a story waits,
A dance of hues, through open gates.
With gentle hands, we tend the soil,
In whispered dreams, our hearts uncoil.

The sun above, it warms our ground,
In every sound, sweet life is found.
With sparkling dew, the morning greets,
In fragrant air, our spirit meets.

Among the petals, hopes are sown,
In gardens lush, our love has grown.
With roots like ours, we intertwine,
In radiant light, our souls align.

As seasons shift and colors change,
The beauty here will rearrange.
Yet in our hearts, the truth remains,
In every storm, love's grace sustains.

So walk with me through green and gold,
In every memory, we unfold.
With laughter shared and tears embraced,
In this sweet haven, life is graced.

Creating a Home in Each Other

In quiet corners, warmth ignites,
With tender hearts, we find our sights.
Each whispered word, a brick we lay,
In cozy rooms, love finds its way.

The laughter echoes through the halls,
In every shadow, our memory calls.
Together we paint, create our space,
In every smile, we find our place.

With open arms, we find our peace,
In every heartbeat, sweet release.
In simple joys, our spirits soar,
Together here, we are much more.

Through storms that shake, through skies that gray,
In each embrace, we choose to stay.
With every glance, and every sigh,
In this love, we learn to fly.

So here we stand, a fortress strong,
Through every trial, we belong.
In every moment, love's design,
Creating home; your heart, my shrine.

Stones of Solace

Beneath the weight of endless days,
We find our peace in quiet ways.
With gentle hands, we place each stone,
In every layer, we are not alone.

Each rocky path tells tales of old,
In silent strength, our hearts are bold.
With every step, we feel the ground,
In nature's pulse, our love is found.

Upon these stones, our memories dwell,
In whispered winds, we cast our spell.
Through every season, rough and smooth,
In solace deep, our spirits soothe.

The river flows, its song so true,
In its embrace, it carries you.
With every turn and twist of fate,
We build our home, we cultivate.

So let the world toss, let it sway,
We find our strength in earth's ballet.
In every stone, a sacred pact,
In stillness found, we both attract.

Heartfelt Construction

With bricks of love we build our dreams,
Foundations strong, or so it seems.
Each laugh a window, bright and wide,
Each tear a door where hope can hide.

Under the roof of whispered fears,
We gather warmth throughout the years.
In every corner, shadows play,
Yet light finds paths to guide the way.

Hammering doubts into the ground,
We lift each other when we're down.
The scaffold bends, but does not break,
Together forged for love's own sake.

Each room a story waiting told,
In every heart, a flame of gold.
As seasons change, our structure stands,
Built on the strength of holding hands.

So here we stand, in life's embrace,
Heartfelt construction, our sacred space.
With every heartbeat, brick and stone,
We build a place we can call home.

Sheltering Souls

In the quiet of the night we find,
A sanctuary where hearts unwind.
Through shadows deep, love's light will pour,
Offering grace, forevermore.

Each gentle breeze whispers your name,
Shelters our souls from all the blame.
In unity, we face the storm,
Wrapped in warmth, forever warm.

The trembling leaves hold secrets true,
Comforting hearts in shades of blue.
Here under stars, dreams intertwine,
In the embrace of hearts that shine.

Together we weather life's fierce trial,
With every setback, we share a smile.
For in this bond, we rise, we soar,
With every moment, we love and explore.

In the end, it's love that creates,
A shelter for our destined fates.
Together we'll tread on paths unknown,
In this world, we'll never be alone.

The Rhythm of Resilient Hearts

In every beat, a story flows,
Resilient hearts, where courage grows.
Each pulse a promise, each thump a vow,
Strength found in moments, here and now.

Life's melody, both sweet and strong,
Carving pathways where we belong.
Through trials faced and mountains climbed,
Rhythm unbroken, spirits aligned.

Like rivers rushing, wild and free,
A symphony of you and me.
We dance to tunes of joy and strife,
The music of our cherished life.

With hands held tight, we'll take the stage,
Persevering through every page.
In moments dark or bright and clear,
The rhythm of love will always steer.

So let it beat, this heart like drum,
For through the chaos, we will come.
In resilient hearts, our stories start,
Crafting anthems, we'll never part.

Cherished Legacies

In whispers soft, our past is spun,
Cherished legacies, one by one.
Each tale a thread woven so tight,
A tapestry of dark and light.

Through hands we hold, and voices warm,
We carry truth throughout the storm.
Lessons learned, both old and new,
Shaping futures, guiding through.

In echoes found that time can't fade,
Heritage blooms, though shadows wade.
With every story shared with grace,
The heart's embrace finds its place.

From seeds we plant in tender grounds,
A legacy in love abounds.
Through laughter shared and tears we shed,
In every moment, our lives are thread.

So let us gather, share our hearts,
Cherished legacies, where life starts.
For in our roots, we find our wings,
In unity, the joy it brings.

Resilient Roots

In the dark earth they dwell, so deep,
Silent strength in stillness keep.
Bending low but never break,
They rise again for hope's own sake.

Through storms that rage and winds that howl,
They anchor firm, respond with growl.
In nature's dance, they sway and bend,
Yet with each dawn, new life they send.

From rocky soil to gentle rain,
Their spirit thrives, untouched by pain.
With every season, they renew,
Resilient hearts, steadfast and true.

In whispered tales of ancient trees,
They speak of strength in gentle breeze.
Roots intertwine, a shared embrace,
United, weathering time and space.

From roots to sky, they rise and grow,
An endless cycle, life's own flow.
Through deepening shadows, light shines through,
Resilience blooms in vibrant hue.

Frameworks of Trust

In quiet moments, promises weave,
A tapestry, where hearts believe.
With threads of hope and care intertwined,
A lasting bond, affection defined.

Through trials faced and laughter shared,
In every glance, a love declared.
A sturdy bridge built strong and wide,
Where vulnerability finds its stride.

Each word a note, a gentle sound,
In harmony, our lives abound.
We nurture faith, like seedlings grow,
In gardens where the trust can flow.

When shadows creep and doubts arise,
In every hug, a sweet surprise.
Together forged, we stand our ground,
In frameworks built on love, we're bound.

With open hearts, we dare to dream,
In unison, we form a team.
Through thick and thin, we've come to know,
That trust, once rooted, will always grow.

The Symphony of Connection

In whispered breezes, voices blend,
A melody that has no end.
Each note a heartbeat, strong and clear,
In harmony, we draw near.

With every laugh and every sigh,
The symphony wraps us, soaring high.
Through shifting tides and changing days,
We find our way in countless ways.

Together we compose the score,
In concert halls, on distant shore.
From shared desires to dreams untold,
A tapestry of hearts grown bold.

As seasons shift and moments glide,
We dance along, hearts open wide.
In gentle rhythms, life unfolds,
A timeless story, rich and bold.

With every sunset, every dawn,
Our connection blooms, forever drawn.
In every heartbeat, every breath,
A symphony that conquers death.

Love's Enduring Canvas

Upon the canvas, colors spread,
With strokes of passion, love is bred.
Each hue a moment, bright and clear,
A masterpiece that draws us near.

With gentle hands, we paint the day,
In laughter's light, in shadows play.
Each line a story, bold and true,
In every layer, me and you.

Through storms that test and winds that shake,
Our art remains, we will not break.
With every challenge, we create,
A vivid portrait, love's own fate.

In afterglow of twilight's kiss,
We find the beauty in the bliss.
With every heartbeat, brush in hand,
Love's canvas grows, a dream so grand.

In timeless strokes, our souls unite,
Creating visions, pure delight.
In every corner, every seam,
A lasting love, forever dream.

The Art of Us

In every stroke, we find a way,
Colors blend as night meets day.
Together, we create the scene,
A masterpiece, so pure and keen.

With laughter's brush, we paint the sky,
In soft pastels, our dreams fly high.
Canvas bright, emotions spread,
In the art of us, all fears are shed.

Your smile, a hue I can't resist,
Each moment shared, a painter's bliss.
Through shadows dark, we craft the light,
In every brushstroke, our spirits ignite.

In silent moments, we find our tone,
Each heartbeat whispers, we're not alone.
Together we flourish, colors merge,
In the art of us, our passions surge.

With every frame, our story grows,
A masterpiece where true love flows.
In this gallery, side by side,
The art of us, a timeless ride.

Threads of Destiny

In every stitch, a tale is spun,
Threads entwined, two hearts as one.
Destiny weaves with gentle hands,
Uniting lives in distant lands.

With golden fibers, paths we trace,
In every knot, a warm embrace.
Through trials faced, our strength is found,
In threads of fate, our love is bound.

Across the tapestry, colors fly,
Woven moments never die.
Each strand holds memories dear,
In threads of destiny, we persevere.

When darkness falls, like shadows cast,
Together we stand, our bond steadfast.
With every loop, our hopes arise,
In timeless weavings, we'll touch the skies.

Our story told in patterns bright,
In every thread, a spark of light.
Hand in hand, forever free,
We weave our fate, just you and me.

Heartprints in the Sand

Beside the waves, we walk and play,
Leaving heartprints along the way.
With every step, our love's embrace,
In golden grains, we find our place.

The tides may wash our marks away,
But memories linger, come what may.
In laughter's echo, shadows cast,
Our heartprints speak of moments past.

With every grain, a story told,
Of dreams we shared and love so bold.
Sunset's glow, a canvas wide,
Our heartprints reveal what's deep inside.

Through storms that roar and skies that weep,
In sandy shores, our promises keep.
Together, we stand, strong and true,
With heartprints forged, just me and you.

As time flows on, we'll still remain,
In every step, through joy and pain.
Though waves may wash the shore so grand,
Our love will leave its heartprints in the sand.

In Harmony We Flourish

In gentle whispers, nature sings,
A symphony of all good things.
Together, roots in earth, we grow,
In harmony, our spirits flow.

With sunlight's embrace and rain's sweet kiss,
We cultivate a world of bliss.
Each leaf and petal, vibrant hue,
In harmony, we thrive anew.

Through seasons' change and trials faced,
Our unity cannot be replaced.
In every struggle, we find our might,
In harmony, we shine so bright.

With open hearts and hands held tight,
We nurture dreams that take to flight.
In the garden of love, we explore,
In harmony, we bloom even more.

As stars align in night's embrace,
Together, we create our space.
In life's grand dance, we find our wish,
In harmony, we flourish, my dearest.

The Mosaic of Us

In colors bright, we weave our tale,
Each piece a story, none too frail.
Together we form a vibrant sight,
A tapestry of love, warm and light.

Fragments scattered, yet aligned,
In chaos found, our hearts combined.
With every shard, a memory grows,
In this mosaic, our true self shows.

Textures unique, we blend with ease,
A harmony that aims to please.
In every crack, a chance to shine,
In imperfections, our love divine.

Colors fade, yet we remain,
Through storms and sun, our joys sustain.
An artwork crafted, bold and free,
The mosaic of you and me.

Together we stand, side by side,
In life's great gallery, our hearts are tied.
With every glance, a silent trust,
Forever bound, in love we rust.

Seasons of Shared Moments

In spring's first bloom, we found our start,
Soft whispers shared, two beating hearts.
Petals dance in the gentle breeze,
Together we laughed beneath the trees.

Summer brought warmth, oh, the sun's romance,
Long glowing days, an endless chance.
With every sunset, our dreams took flight,
Under starlit skies, we held on tight.

As autumn leaves began to fall,
We gathered memories, cherished all.
The crisp air wrapped us, side by side,
In golden hues, our love with pride.

Winter's chill may cover the ground,
But in our hearts, warmth can be found.
Through swirling snow, we find our way,
In quiet moments, our love will stay.

Seasons shift, yet we endure,
In every moment, our bond stays pure.
The cycle spins, but through it all,
Hand in hand, we shall not fall.

Golden Threads

Through time we stitch, with threads so gold,
A tapestry rich, with stories bold.
Every knot a promise, every loop a vow,
Crafting our future, here and now.

In laughter bright, and whispers low,
These golden threads of love do grow.
Woven tightly, our hearts reside,
In this fabric, we take great pride.

Every tear a lesson, every seam a chance,
To mend and nurture, to love and dance.
In threads of gold, our hopes we thread,
A masterpiece, in joy, we're led.

With every stitch, a moment shared,
Every breath taken, every thought declared.
Soft and sturdy, the ties that bind,
In this golden tapestry, our souls aligned.

Forever woven, in colors bright,
Each golden thread, a shining light.
In this fabric, our love will grow,
A warm embrace in every glow.

The Path to Togetherness

On winding trails, our journey starts,
Two wandering souls, with open hearts.
Through forests deep and mountains high,
We walk this path, just you and I.

In every step, a story unfolds,
Hand in hand, our love upholds.
With every turn, discoveries made,
In laughter and joy, our worries fade.

Rivers to cross, and bridges to build,
Together we stand, with dreams fulfilled.
A compass of trust, guiding us near,
Our hearts the map, with love sincere.

Through rocky paths, the sun may hide,
Yet side by side, we'll never slide.
In storms that rage, we find our calm,
In each other's arms, we're safe, we're warm.

As the horizon beckons, a new dawn breaks,
With every moment, our promise wakes.
Together we find our way, it's true,
The path to togetherness, me and you.

Eternal Embrace

In the quiet glow of the dawn,
Two souls entwined, never to part.
A love that defies the hands of time,
Wrapped in warmth, heart to heart.

With each soft sigh that fills the air,
Promises whispered, a sacred pact.
Through shadows cast and light laid bare,
Together, they stand, unbroken, intact.

The stars above, their destiny,
Guiding their path through the night.
In gentle winds, they find their way,
An eternal embrace, pure delight.

Though the seasons may come and go,
Their bond remains a timeless sea.
In storms and calms, forever strong,
Two hearts dance in sweet harmony.

In each fleeting moment, love glows bright,
A tapestry woven with threads of gold.
An eternal embrace, their hearts ignite,
In stories of old, forever told.

Tapestry of Togetherness

Threads of laughter, colors bright,
Woven tightly, heart to heart.
Each moment shared, a gleaming light,
Creating a masterpiece, a joyful art.

Through highs and lows, they stand as one,
In every stitch, a tale to share.
In the warmth of love, like the sun,
Crafting a tapestry beyond compare.

With hands interlaced, they paint the sky,
Brushstrokes of dreams on canvas wide.
In every embrace, the reason why,
Together, they flourish, side by side.

Life's vibrant hues, both bold and soft,
Each thread a memory to hold close.
In the fabric of days, they lift each other,
A tapestry of togetherness, love engrossed.

So let us weave with care and grace,
A story of unity, tender and true.
In this tapestry, find your place,
Together forever, me and you.

The Bridge of Time

Across the river where dreams reside,
A bridge stands tall, transcending fate.
With whispers of love, side by side,
They traverse the years, never late.

Each step they take, a journey shared,
Moments captured in the tapestry.
Their laughter echoes, hearts laid bare,
Creating memories, wild and free.

In the twilight glow, shadows grow,
Yet hand in hand, they fear no end.
For in their hearts, a timeless flow,
The bridge of time, forever a friend.

With courage found in every glance,
They dance through storms, face the night.
In the depths of silence, they find romance,
The bridge of time, their guiding light.

And as the stars begin to fade,
They stand together, strong and pure.
In the bridge of time, love's serenade,
An eternal bond, forever sure.

Whispers in the Wind

Among the trees, where secrets dwell,
Whispers in the wind softly call.
A song of love, enchanting spell,
Carried through leaves, a gentle thrall.

In twilight's hush, they share a glance,
Soft murmurs wrapped in twilight's glow.
With every breath, they weave a dance,
In the soft embrace of the evening's flow.

The echoes of laughter fill the air,
A melody played on a silken string.
In turbulent times, they're always there,
Whispers in the wind, love's offering.

Through valleys low and mountains high,
Their spirits soar, wild and free.
With hearts unchained, they touch the sky,
In whispers, they find their harmony.

So listen close, let your heart unwind,
For love has a language, soft and sweet.
In every breeze, a story you'll find,
Whispers in the wind, where hearts meet.

Hearth of Our Hopes

In the glow of soft embers,
Dreams flicker, ignite high.
Warmth wraps around us tight,
In this space where we sigh.

Whispers dance in the night,
Promises linger in air.
Together we chase the light,
Binding hearts with sweet care.

Moments gleam like the stars,
Winds carry our soft laughs.
Through trouble, we roam far,
Always finding our paths.

Voices weave through the dark,
Sharing secrets, our fears.
In this home, love's the spark,
Burning bright through the years.

Together we rise above,
Each challenge a chance to grow.
In the hearth, we find love,
Fueling dreams as we flow.

The Quilt of Commitment

Stitched with threads of our vows,
Colors blend, intertwine here.
Each patch tells stories proud,
Over time they draw near.

With every fold, a moment,
Laughter woven with tears.
In the fabric, our content,
Embracing all the years.

Guarded lines mark the strife,
Yet brightness always shines.
In this quilt, we find life,
A tapestry that binds.

Each corner holds a memory,
Stitches placed with intention.
Together we weave history,
In love's warm dimension.

So wrap me in this embrace,
Where every thread is true.
In commitment, we find grace,
Our quilt forever new.

Every Brick a Memory

Each brick laid with intention,
Stories carved deep within.
Foundations of our affection,
Holding up where we've been.

Walls echo every laughter,
Chiseled into each space.
Through heartache and sweet after,
In this home, love found place.

Rooftops shelter our dreams,
As seasons shift and sway.
In every hand-crafted seam,
Memories hold at bay.

Windows shine with bright futures,
Reflecting all that we share.
In the stillness, our features,
Carved in timeless repair.

With each dawn, new layers,
Unfolding what we possess.
In each brick, our prayers,
This home, our happiness.

The Flow of Forever

Time dances like a river,
Carrying our shared dreams.
In its flow, we find shiver,
Yet warmth in love's sweet beams.

Every moment, a ripple,
Echoes through our own hearts.
In this journey, we triple,
As our story imparts.

As the water runs freely,
Together we drift along.
In its current, we see,
Life's a beautiful song.

Through valleys and to the peaks,
The tides will always find way.
With each wave, joy speaks,
In the dawn of each day.

So let us flow like the tide,
Unfettered, wild, and true.
In the depths, heart's our guide,
Forever, just me and you.

Milton Keynes UK
Ingram Content Group UK Ltd.
UKHW021033021124
450589UK00013B/897